Love You to Death

Elizabeth Ruth

Love You to Death

Grass Roots Press

Grass Roots Press gratefully acknowledges the financial support for its publishing programs provided by the following agencies: the Government of Canada through the Canada Book Fund and the Government of Alberta through the Alberta Foundation for the Arts.

Grass Roots Press would also like to thank ABC Life Literacy Canada for their support. Good Reads® is used under licence from ABC Life Literacy Canada.

Library and Archives Canada Cataloguing in Publication

Ruth, Elizabeth, author
    Love you to death / Elizabeth Ruth.

(Good reads)
ISBN 978-1-77153-002-6 (pbk.)

    1. Readers for new literates. I. Title. II. Series: Good reads series (Edmonton, Alta.)

PS8585.U847L69 2013   428.6'2   C2013-902653-3

Printed and bound in Canada.

All the lonely people, where do they all come from?

—The Beatles

Chapter One

"You seem tense, Ivy," Dr. Stamp said.

"Am I?" I said. "I mean, do I?" I've always had trouble with my thoughts and feelings. Going to see a therapist once a week was supposed to help me with these problems.

I glanced around Dr. Stamp's office. There was a large desk. A phone. A cup full of pens and a pad of lined paper. A water cooler stood in the corner. Then I looked at Dr. Stamp, sitting behind his desk. He is a short, chubby man. He speaks with fancy words and really seems to care about my mental health. But I knew what he was thinking: that I only imagine no one likes me.

"Maybe I'm tense about my birthday next month," I said. "I'll be thirty."

Dr. Stamp lowered his chin and looked at me over the top of his glasses. "Are you still writing down thoughts in your journal?" he asked. "Are you going to the gym?"

"Sometimes," I lied.

*

My friend Robin and I had joined a health club near the office. Working out together was easier than doing exercise alone. We'd tried classes. Step and spinning classes. Pilates, when it was the new craze. But ever since Robin became pregnant, she's been afraid to put any stress on her body. So I've lost my gym buddy.

Robin and Phil are the happiest couple I know. No, they are the *only* happy couple I know. They've been together for four years. Then last year mommy-fever hit Robin like a piano falling from a skyscraper. She decided to join everyone else our age in an act of—*ta-da!*—tradition. Robin and Phil's wedding was sweet and old-fashioned. They invited only close friends and family. I agreed to be the maid of honour, as long as I could choose my dress. Liz organized the bridal shower.

Liz is my other friend. She's a literary agent who helps writers sell the stories they write. A natural blond, she has a thin face and high cheekbones. She's beautiful, but here's what everyone remembers about her looks. One of her eyes is green and the other eye is pale blue. I often feel the blue one is watching me most closely.

Liz has strong opinions about what kinds of books are worth reading. She sees books as high art, full of big ideas—the type that make a person's head hurt. The thought that most people like to read for fun wouldn't occur to her. "I never touch ordinary books, like romances, mysteries, and thrillers," she often says. She sounds offended, as if we were asking the queen to wash her own windows. "They're a waste of trees!" she says. "I won't read them."

Not Robin. Robin speaks up when Liz makes fun of the books she works on. Robin is an editor. Her job is to make sure writers have said exactly what they want to say, and said it properly. She's the youngest editor Pages & Print Books has ever hired.

"My thrillers are the hottest books on the market," Robin says when Liz gets all self-important.

But I know for a fact Robin is worried that stories about serial killers are going out of fashion. She told me. She has no reason to worry, though. People with disturbed minds never really go out of style.

✱

A few years ago, I introduced Robin and Phil. I had met Phil in 2008 at a party for one of Liz's writers. Phil told me he was a doctor, the sort who helps women get pregnant. I tried to make small talk, but I'm not very good at that. I let Phil do most of the talking. He asked what I did for a living. Liz, who likes to be dramatic, came along just then and heard his question. She told him I guard the gates at Pages & Print Books.

"Really? *She* doesn't look scary enough," Phil said. He looked Liz up and down. At her tightly pulled-back hair, the mink collar of her dress, her spike heels. "But you do!"

I laughed out loud, the way my half-sister, Cara, would have laughed. Anybody who calls Liz's bluff impresses me.

Phil and I shared a cab home that night. We made out in the back seat. The driver watched us in the rear-view mirror. Phil's hands were soft and greedy.

Robin knows about the taxi ride. She's okay with it. Once she even asked me why I didn't try to get Phil for myself. I didn't know what to tell her. The thing is, Phil is very confident. Sure of himself. I can never tell what self-possessed men are thinking. And he spends his life bringing babies into the world for people who want them. He's almost a god. Someone like me could never hold on to someone like him.

Phil did leave a couple of phone messages after the taxi ride, though. I didn't return his calls.

Months later, Robin and I ran into him at a coffee shop. He had on the same wrinkled navy suit. I noticed the same coffee-coloured eyes. And those greedy, healing hands. Now Robin and Phil live in High Park, in a great big house facing the pond. Not in a dumpy apartment like mine.

Chapter Two

Robin was hired as an editor at Pages & Print Books straight out of university. She had studied drama. She knew nothing about publishing books. In fact, she had hardly any work history at all. But the boss, Jack Holland, liked her sense of style and her timing. (She was half an hour early for the interview.)

I like her because she's trusting. You don't find many trusting people anymore. Everyone is so busy acting as if they know everything.

Robin looks the way you might expect someone with that name to look. She's fine-boned, just like a bird. Used to be a ballet dancer. Her hair is short and wispy, like blue-black feathers around her face, and she wears red lipstick. I've often caught her singing to herself. We're the same age. Like me, she would rather work in a pair of blue jeans and a ratty old T-shirt. But, also like me, she suffers, day after day, in heels and dry-cleaned suits. Publishing books is mostly a female profession. Women try hard to get ahead of each other. Maybe that's why being well-dressed and good-looking seems like an Olympic sport.

Robin and I have a lot in common. For one thing, we both work at Pages & Print Books. For another, neither of us secretly wants to write the great Canadian novel. We are readers. And from the time I *could* read, I've read fairy tales, fiction, and horror. Just the sorts of books we publish. Thrillers filled with mind games and dark, empty lives—they're my favourites.

Hundreds, even thousands of writers send their work to our company. They hope someone will like it well enough to turn it into a book. We call our mountain of mail the "slush pile." The name isn't very nice, but it does describe most of what is sent in by hopeful writers.

I'm the one who goes through all that mail. I make sure only the best book ideas get in. Then I hand what I find to Robin. She's paid to know what will send shivers up readers' backs. And she gets all the credit. Maybe it's not fair, but I'm just Ivy Moore, full-time receptionist. Robin gets to decide what will climb the bestseller lists.

*

"Phil called me at work today," I told Dr. Stamp during our next session. "Robin is usually the one who phones me, but Phil made a point of calling me himself. He and Robin want *me* to be the baby's godmother."

"How wonderful!" said Dr. Stamp.

I felt my chest tighten. "I could never in a million years take care of a child. And I can't see myself as any kind of mother. The only thing I've ever helped to grow is the mould inside my fridge."

"*Ivy.*"

"Okay, maybe I put it too strongly. But I'm not exactly mother material. Not even godmother material."

"Is that what you told Phil?"

"No, of course not. I told him yes, and thank you. I mean, it's an honour. Right?" I crossed my legs and looked at the carpet.

Truth is, I've never been comfortable when someone says something nice to me. I feel I don't deserve it. I always think it must be a mistake. If only the person really knew me.

✱

One day back in late July, Robin leaned across my desk. "Let's celebrate tonight," she said. "Phil has an old friend in town."

"Forget it." I slid my chair away from her, tidied some papers. "The last guy you set me up with called the Leaning Tower of Pisa 'the leaning tower of pizza.'"

"This one's a professor. He and Phil have known each other since their university days. He's very cute. I *swear*. You'll love him."

I was silent. Love is only for special people, people like Robin and Phil. People who know how to share.

"Please?" said Robin. "He's been divorced for a year and hasn't dated much."

I gave in. That evening I met Robin, Phil, and their friend at a nearby restaurant. I wore a grey pencil skirt, cut just below the knee, and a pale pink blouse. When I swung open the second set of doors, I noticed a run in my nylons. I couldn't go home and change because Phil and Robin were standing right there, waiting for me.

"Phil's friend isn't here yet," Robin said, squeezing my arm. The waitress led us to a round red leather booth at the back. My outfit looked dull in the rich gold and red room.

Just as we were about to sit down, a tall man in his late thirties, maybe early forties, appeared at Phil's side. He was wearing a pair of blue jeans and a soft blue sweater. Big smile. "Hey, buddy," he said, slapping Phil on the back. He slid into the booth between Robin and me. "You must be Ivy," he said, extending his hand. "I'm Mark."

I shook his hand and smiled.

"You're right, Robin," he said. "She *is* beautiful."

I blushed and kicked Robin under the table. I'm nothing to look at, not compared to other women. My eyes are a dull copper colour and my skin is too pale. My thin straight hair is brown and cut into a pageboy. The style suits the shape of my wide, shiny face, at least.

"So, you and Phil go way back?" I asked.

Mark pushed up his sleeves. Short, light brown hair covered his muscular arms. "Almost twenty years, I guess. We met during our first week of university. A bunch of us got so drunk we camped on the lawn."

Camping. All at once, I could see my half-sister Cara. She was as clear to me as if she were standing in front of me. I felt as if I had gone back in time. I was sitting in the dark on a cliff above Looking Glass Lake. Powerless, with a scream trapped inside my throat.

I reached for my water glass. It was empty. I hid my shaky hands in my lap under the table, wiping them on my skirt. What's most interesting about fear is how it comes back, year after year. The body remembers.

Robin poked me. "Ivy?"

Everyone at the table stared.

"Oh, sorry." I wiped the film of sweat from my upper lip. "My mind was far away."

I made it through the appetizers without acting strange. By the time the main course arrived, my memories of Cara had faded. I could carry on a decent conversation.

Mark had to send his meal back to the kitchen because the food had crushed peanuts on top. He's terribly allergic to peanuts, he told us. Eating the smallest bit of peanut could make him sick enough to die.

While Mark waited for a different meal, he shared some of my fish. I enjoyed the smooth, deep sound of his voice. He spoke well, and he knew how to tell a good story.

When Robin and I went to the washroom before dessert, Robin dropped the bomb. "Mark's university has let him go. He has taken a job teaching history here, at the University of Toronto," she said. "He'll start in the fall. But he needs a place to stay for a month while he waits for his condo to be ready."

Robin pulled a lipstick out of her purse and faced the mirror. "Our house is a mess because of work on the baby's room." I watched her put on more lipstick and tried to imagine Mark on my pullout couch. Robin closed her lips over a tissue. "You like him, Ivy. I can tell."

Chapter Three

I was in bed, reading, when the doorbell rang. I threw off the covers and slipped into my robe. I flipped the light switch in the hall. Through the peephole in the door, Mark's head looked larger than his body. I unbolted the door.

"You're sopping wet," I said. "The rain must be pouring down."

He shook out of his coat and tossed it across the radiator. "Listen, I know we agreed that I wouldn't move in until the weekend. But I had to get out of that hotel. There's an all-night rave going on in the room next door. It's too noisy. I have a meeting with my new boss at nine in the morning. I need sleep so I don't make a fool of myself."

My heart pounded a little faster. "Now or the weekend—it doesn't make any difference."

Mark dropped a garment bag and his briefcase on the floor. "Ivy, you're a life saver."

I came back a few minutes later with a clean set of sheets and a pillow. Mark had taken off everything but his boxer shorts and a T-shirt. He was asleep sitting up on my couch, his elbow on its arm, his chin in his hand. His shoes and socks were piled on the green shag rug at his feet. His damp sweater and jeans lay beside them. Even in that relaxed state, his thighs were muscular, his stomach flat under his shirt. His skin was waxy and pale. He reminded me of one of Dad's dead bodies after he was done embalming it at the funeral home.

I covered Mark with the sheets—except for his head. I set the pillow on the coffee table. Then I checked the bolt on the door and flicked off the lights. I tiptoed back down the hall. When I climbed into my bed, my chest felt tight. *Mark's very handsome*, I thought. *And he needs me.*

I lay in bed staring at the ceiling. *What would it feel like to have Mark sleeping next to me?* I thought about his large hands. I could already feel interest bubbling up between us—even if he couldn't. His garment bag now hung in my hall closet. The suit in it made a perfect shadow of him behind the door.

I finally fell asleep, but I woke a few hours later. I felt as if someone was on top of me, pushing right through me. But no one was there, just me.

Dr. Stamp says we need to explore my dreams further. He always wants to know what's in them. Me, I don't believe dreams have meaning. I don't believe in healing the "inner child." I don't believe in any explanations of the mind at all. I'm just plain frigid. Frigid Ivy. Try saying that ten times fast. *FrigidIvyfrigidIvyfrigidIvy.*

Frigid is my word, not Dr. Stamp's. He thinks I'm afraid of intimacy, and my fear won't let me get close to anyone. But I know something he doesn't. I know it's not only houses that are haunted. Sometimes people are haunted, too.

In the morning, Mark's sweater and pants lay folded in one corner of my living room. His coat was no longer drying on the radiator. I felt disappointed that he'd left before I woke up.

I'd never had a man sleep over before. I was looking forward to the man-things that Liz and Robin complained about. Shaving cream and tiny whiskers in the bathroom sink. My toilet seat up.

The sports section of the paper spread out across the kitchen table. Mark had dashed off, barely leaving a trace. *Maybe I dreamed him*, I thought.

Before my half-sister, Cara, came to live with my parents and me, I'd only had imaginary friends. I made up adventures and got lost inside my own mind. Each of my dolls had names and fully formed personalities. By the time I was four, I'd killed them off, stuffed and re-stuffed them. I had pretended to be Dad at the funeral home, taking care of dead bodies. You know how it is? You know what they say? Only child, lonely child.

I dragged myself to the bathroom and into a hot shower. I noticed a new bar of soap in a plastic travel box. *Mark*, I thought, reaching for it. My belly fluttered. I held the soap under my nose. It smelled athletic, zesty. It was the kind Dad used to wash the stink of chemicals and death from his skin after an embalming. I soaped myself all over. Afterwards, I lifted Mark's terry cloth robe from the hook. I slipped into it as if I was slipping into someone else's skin.

Chapter Four

I arrived late to work. Most of my co-workers were in the board room with the door closed. As I hurried towards my desk, Robin opened the door. She waved for me to join them.

"Big news, Ivy. It's about *The Fallen Affair*."

"Be right there," I said.

I dropped my bag and fished under my desk for a dry pair of shoes. *The Fallen Affair* was our most important book last fall. I was still getting calls about it, too often from the author himself. I had found the typed pages in the slush pile among all the hopeless, silly work that writers had sent the company. I saw that the story was great, but the writing was terrible. I told Robin that the book would be her blockbuster. She couldn't see that at first. But I made her believe it, even though she had to make tons of changes.

We all believed our work would pay off, and it did. *The Fallen Affair* became a bestseller right away. Then, just like its title, it fell, and fast. (Come to think of it, that title was a poor choice.) A few newspaper and magazine writers liked the book. One review even praised *The Fallen Affair* for "lifting the thriller to a new level." But most of the reviews were not as good. In fact, a lot of them were terrible.

The book was brilliant, though. I had known that right away. *The Fallen Affair* was the perfect blend of popular fiction and pretty language. The sort of thing that sells like hot cakes these days.

Sam Roddin, the author, was the sort of man who could put you off reading his work. Even at twenty-five years old, he was a proud, cigar-smoking phony. All of us younger women would suddenly find his chubby hands on our bottoms. But he was very talented. We knew Sam would make Pages & Print Books into a star of the book publishing world. Liz, of course, was his agent.

At my desk, I pulled off one wet shoe and then the other. I struggled out of my nylons. My soft belly rubbed against the material of my skirt. I felt as fat as Robin looked at seven and a half months pregnant. *Must get back to the gym*, I thought. I grabbed a pen and my day planner and headed down the hall.

When I opened the board room door, everyone stopped talking. Jack Holland, the publisher and our boss, sat at the end of the long wooden table. Robin sat beside Jack, bursting at the seams with excitement. Liz was there, too.

"What's so important?" I said. Did they know about the box of books I'd sent to my apartment without paying for them?

"Well," said Liz. "Whatever it is, it better not be dead, drunk, or in the mood to sue."

A junior editor pushed a chair my way. I sat. *Jack's smiling*, I thought. *Something's definitely wrong.*

"*The Fallen Affair* has won the Yorkie Award!" said Jack. Then he pulled Robin up out of her chair as if she were a swollen rag doll. "You did it, sweetheart. You saw how good that book was from the get-go. Never mind those idiot reviewers! We've got ourselves a winner after all."

"Do you know what this means?" said someone from sales. "Robin's going to get the editor-of-the-year award for sure."

Robin thrust a copy of an e-mail my way. The message had been sent only minutes before. "Bravo, Ms. O'Brien!" it said. "We hope you'll join our table on awards night." It was signed by Trudy Penn. She was the president of Penn's, the largest bookstore chain in the country.

I was speechless. Every pore in my skin opened to light and air and sound. I felt a headache coming on. Sure, Robin had fixed up the book, but *I* had been the one to pull it out of the slush pile. *I* was the first one to lay eyes on the envelope. Then, when I read the typed pages, *I* had seen its brilliance. *Me!*

"The Yorkie?" I finally said. "Way to go."

"Biggest award in the country," said Jack. He rubbed his hands together.

Robin beamed. She couldn't believe her luck. "You find a story with great promise," she said. "You hope to shape the story into a good book. You hope the book will draw attention. You just don't ever know for sure."

Liz glanced around the table. "Does Sam know?" No one answered, so Liz stood. "I'd better go tell him before the press gets to him. We don't want Sam shooting his mouth off."

"Let Ivy do it," said Jack. He gave Robin a squeeze. "We're going out for lunch to celebrate."

Chapter Five

After work, Robin and I met Liz on the outdoor patio at Le Bistro. "Larry King wants the US television interview with Sam," Robin said.

Liz lit a cigarette. "I heard. And Jack wants you on TV with Sam."

"You?" I said to Robin. "On Larry King?"

"I know. Look at me," said Robin. "On TV I'll look like a hot-air balloon."

"Jack's worried about Sam shooting his mouth off," said Liz. "Remember the last time he was on TV? He made the entire west coast mad. Robin can control him. Even Sam agrees it's a good idea, and he doesn't like to share the spotlight." Liz lifted her glass of brandy. "Sam Roddin's a weasel. No, make that a rat. I told you both as much when I signed him up as a client. God love him. That fool is going to make us all rich."

"Liz," I said, "you sure have a way of putting things."

I'd been on my way to work the morning I met Liz for the first time. I had pulled up in a cab next to the office, and I was fishing in my purse for a ten-dollar bill. She'd tapped on the window. "In or out?" she said. She was wearing her usual white blouse, white pants, no make-up. Liz is the type who'd never order special licence plates for her car, if she had a car. Never wear blue eye shadow, earmuffs, or her heart on her sleeve. But fur? In a second.

That morning, when she opened her mouth to speak, out came this strong New York accent. It swallowed everything around it. Right away, I saw her sense of her own importance. "I'm in a rush," she'd added. "Do you mind?"

You just have to accept Liz. She's the kind of woman who would never swim backstroke. She needs to see where she's going at all times. She storms through life. Walking fast, a lit cigarette in hand. Liz does everything boldly. No air of doubt. No hesitation. She gives me hope.

A sharp laugh from Liz brought me back to our conversation. The thought of being on TV with Sam had Robin feeling worried, for sure.

"Get Jack to do the interview," I said. "If you don't want to."

Liz lit the second of the evening's long line of Rothmans extra mild. "Jack likes Sam," she agreed.

"You always say you're a behind-the-scenes kind of person," I added.

"See?" said Robin. "Even Ivy thinks I'll flub."

"The crew will make you look gorgeous," said Liz. "Don't worry, the whole yummy-mummy thing is in style. Find a few things to highlight about the book. And I can talk to Sam, if you want. I'll tell him that if he says something stupid he can find another agent."

Liz laughed again and took a heavy drag on her cigarette. She blew a smoke ring across the table. "Just talk about how much everyone at Pages & Print loves the book. Sam will cover the writing angle. Make something up. Talk about how you met while building an igloo or hunting for moose. Americans eat up that northern stuff."

"Jesus, Liz." Robin coughed and waved her hand. "Do you have to smoke around me?"

"Let's talk about something else," I said.

"Good idea." Robin moved her hand over her belly in wide, gentle circles. "I feel sick to my stomach."

"I thought morning sickness ended after the first few months," said Liz.

"Usually it does. But not with me. With me it's been this constant reminder that I have company."

Company. That was the word she used. As if she were talking about some out-of-town guest!

"It sounds more like a hostile takeover," said Liz.

"I'm ignoring that." Robin's face glowed. She'd turned into one of *those* mothers-to-be. It happened the instant she read the blue stripe on her home pregnancy test. You know the type? Shows you her belly. Places your hand there so you can feel movement. Is proud of the stretch marks. "I'm telling you," she said. "All those cheesy articles you read in women's magazines? They're true. I feel powerful. I've never felt this much love for anyone before. Not even Phil."

Liz shook her head. "Sperm meets egg and suddenly a soul mate is along for the ride? Ugh! Remind me to get my tubes tied."

"Ignore her, Ivy," Robin said. "You'll feel the same when it happens to you."

"It's not going to happen to me," I said in a small voice. "I'll be thirty soon. I'm still single." I felt ashamed saying that word out loud: "single," as if I were confessing some terrible sin. As if being single is the lowest state of being for any living thing. Double is what we all want to be, isn't it?

"You've got time," Robin said. She squeezed my hand across the table. "Being pregnant does change everything. Little things. That's the wildest part. Like, I'll be at home doing my taxes or trying to sleep, when bam! The baby's wide awake and living his own life."

Liz called our waiter over. "Excuse me, is the food coming? My friend needs to eat." Liz turned to us. "There, now. I hate to break up this bonding session, but I have something *important* to share." Liz tilted her head and blew smoke into the air. "Ladies, I'm in love." She waved her hand around in front of my face. A trail of smoke hovered over my empty dinner plate. "Hello? Anybody there? I said, I'm in love."

"With yourself?" Robin asked. She winked at me.

Liz flicked the ash of her cigarette into an ashtray. "Funny, mamma mia." She leaned in to me. "His name is Rafael. Rafe for short. He's ab-so-lute-ly precious."

"Let me guess," said Robin. "Rich. Tall. Curly dark hair. Eye colour, who cares. Good in bed. And married?"

"Unmarried." Liz said.

"Divorced?"

"A bachelor. No children. Most important, he *adores* me."

"Sounds like a match made in heaven," said Robin. "But I don't get why you're attracted to him. I mean, if he's available."

"They're all available, sweetie."

Our waiter appeared, holding three large plates. Liz took a long last drag on her cigarette.

Sometimes Liz reminds me of my half-sister, Cara. Not just her me-me-me attitude, but the way she treats men. She makes some guy think he's the centre of the universe, then she dumps him. For Liz, men are like costume jewelry at a yard sale. She was married once in her early twenties. Spur-of-the-moment kind of thing. It didn't last out the year. She has always said she's not made for long-term plans. So why be in love?

"Would it bother you if Rafe was with another woman?" I asked.

"No." Liz shook her head. "I want my freedom, too."

I didn't believe her. She has a cell phone full of men's numbers and only two close female friends.

Which reminded me: I should ask Dr. Stamp what makes a friendship a close one. I mean, am I close enough with my friends?

Chapter Six

Cara had always known about me, about our family. Where our house was. That Dad embalmed dead people for a living. I heard my parents shouting at each other before she came to live with us. Dad said he was sorry, over and over. That his affair with Cara's mother was all a big mistake. He didn't even know about Cara until the call came from social services. Mum said she didn't think she could forgive him. She didn't want to raise another woman's child. How could she love Cara?

One night, I had my ear pressed against their bedroom door, and Dad caught me. He had swung open the door, ready to storm downstairs and out of the house. "You've got a sister," he said. "Get used to it!" Mum buried her head in her pillow and sobbed.

Then, on the afternoon of my ninth birthday, Dad walked Cara into the dining room. He sat her down at the table. Mum had just started to sing "Happy Birthday." She gritted her teeth and smiled. "Everyone, this is Cara," she said to my school friends. "I want you to make her feel welcome."

Cara was a year younger than me. She took after her mother. Long blond hair and bright green eyes, olive skin. She had skinny arms and legs. Even though she was only eight, she was taller than me. I've always been pretty short.

Marsha Crawford, Cara's real mother, died in a car crash. It happened on Highway 11 outside of Huntsville, where they lived. Cara saw the glare of headlights coming at them like sharp white teeth. She saw the terror on her mother's face during her last seconds, saw the bloody mess of her limp body. She told me about it. Social services took her into care and began to look for a new home for her. Cara's uncle was in Japan teaching English as a second language, and her grandparents lived in a seniors home. Cara's mother had told Cara's granny Dad's name. That's how Cara's granny knew what to tell the woman from social services.

Turned out that Dad had first met Marsha, Cara's mother, at a ski hotel one winter. He was up there for a weekend meeting about embalming bodies. Marsha worked in the restaurant, waiting on tables. She was beautiful, with the kind of beauty I can't imagine having. The kind that would make men sell their souls just to have you once.

*

"The whole pregnancy thing is a little bit weird for me," I told Dr. Stamp. "I mean, I'm happy for Robin and Phil. Well, I try to be. But the idea of something taking over my body, I find that scary. I'm going to be the baby's godmother. What if I pass along my ... hang-ups?"

"Is this really about your trust issues?" Dr. Stamp asked.

I nodded.

"Okay, let's start again. What's the first thing that comes to mind when I say 'man'?"

"Male."

"Yes," Dr. Stamp tried not to sigh. "Then what?"

The only thing that came to my mind was Dad. So I said, "My father."

"Ah, good."

"I guess. It's just that you say 'male' and I think, hmm... A beard, too much time spent at work. Cheating."

"We've been over this, Ivy. You think all men cheat."

"Liz is having another affair," I said. The force in my voice took us both by surprise.

"Liz? Oh, your agent friend."

"This is her third in six months."

"Is there a limit?"

"No, but this time she says she's *in love.*"

"That's what's bothering you? She might have found real intimacy?"

"It's not fair. Robin has a great job, and she has Phil. Soon she'll have the baby. She doesn't know how lucky she is. Liz has a pile of money and now some guy named Rafe. I'm alone. It's so easy for them. They just reach out and take what they want."

"Your friends are moving on with their lives. You feel left behind."

"Wouldn't you?"

"Isn't there anyone you're interested in?"

I shook my head. "Oh, wait. Maybe. His name is Mark. He's an old friend of Phil's, that's all. He needed a place to stay for a month. I offered my pullout couch."

"That was very kind of you." Dr. Stamp pushed his glasses back up onto the bridge of his nose. "You have someone you're attracted to living in your apartment. You don't know how to handle that. Liz would. Robin would. You don't."

"He's not living there exactly, and there's nothing to handle!" I hate it when a therapist thinks he knows everything.

"So you're not interested in Mark, and he's not interested in you."

"Well, he did ask me out to dinner. That was just to be polite. I said no."

"Of course, because you don't find him attractive."

"I didn't say that. Is that what I said?" I folded my arms across my chest. "He probably has lots of women," I added, thinking of Rafe and Liz. Thinking of Dad and Marsha Crawford.

"So what if he does?"

I clenched my jaw. "That won't work," I said. "I have to be the only one."

*

My parents still live in the house I grew up in. It's at 126 Baylor Avenue, right near the bottom of a dead end street. I could see the Mount Pleasant cemetery out my bedroom window. After Cara moved in, she would sit on the wide ledge at night with the window open. "You can hear them breathing," she'd say about the people buried there. I'd look. The graves seemed to inhale and exhale, rise and fall, under the well-cut grass.

Sometimes we'd jump the fence and wander through the cemetery. Cara was brave. She'd step across the plots. I'd only walk around them. Headstones and half-dug graves were our toys. No more lonely games or imaginary friends for me, once Cara arrived. I had her, and the dead ones.

We both knew the names of all the people buried within half a kilometre of our house. For each grave, Cara made up a story to explain what had killed the person. A plastic bag over the head. Hunger. Rare disease. You name it and she'd thought it up.

"You're gross," I once said.

"Death is gross."

Mum seemed to catch on early: there was something not quite right about Cara. She tried to warn my father. "She laughs when people get hurt, John. She never cries."

"She needs a stable home," Dad said flatly. He could have been talking about one of his corpses. Like, "This one needs a more natural smile," or "This one needs to be dressed."

Once, in grade nine, I drank half a bottle of rum on a dare. I did it so some idiot friend of Cara's could feel me up. The two of them spun me around in the graveyard. They unbuttoned my top so the lace of my bra was showing. Whatever his name was, he shoved his hand into my bra. I fell and hit my head. Woke up in a partly dug grave, where Cara had put me. I threw up for three days straight. Cara told Dad that I had food poisoning from bad takeout food.

Dad believed her. I wanted to tell him what had really happened. I didn't. I was starting to think maybe Dad loved Cara more than he loved me. In fact, I knew he did.

Chapter Seven

I knew Mark and I were soul mates after our first week of living together. At work, I drew us holding hands, him giving me a diamond ring, me in my wedding dress. Then I put the drawings through the shredder. On Saturday, my thirtieth birthday, Mark said he was going to the library. I wandered through the mall, looking at maternity clothes. Feeling hopeful, I bought a nursing bra. Then I took a cab home. *Maybe Mark will stay in tonight*, I thought.

I struggled with my key in the door. When I pushed inside, the lights flashed on. I blinked. Robin was jumping up and down, holding her belly. She looked like a giant version of the blue and silver balloons tied to my floor lamp. Streamers hung from the ceiling. A large red banner stuck to the wall said "Happy Birthday!" Phil waved from behind my kitchen table.

Mark stood beside the couch in the exact spot where he'd stood the night he moved in. *So tall*, I thought. *Good bones*. A few others from work were there. Liz stood by an open window, smoking. She waved with a cigarette between her fingers. For a moment I was afraid to enter my own home. Robin guided me in. Someone turned music on.

"You look stunned," said Liz. She turned to Robin. "I told you. Some people don't like surprises."

"It's just … I didn't expect…" I tried to smile. "I don't know what to say."

"Say 'grape' or 'cherry,'" Phil called from the kitchen. He was holding up a martini glass.

"Cherry," I answered.

Mark pulled a bouquet of red and yellow tulips out from behind his back. He kissed me on the cheek. I could feel the hot outline of his lips on my skin.

"Oh, don't let *him* steal all the glory," said Liz. She grabbed the bouquet away. "We chipped in and got you something that will live longer than a week."

Phil came out of the kitchen with my martini. "You don't look a day over thirty."

"*God*, Philip," said Liz. "Must you remind her of her age? Ivy, take it from me, now's a good time to begin lying about that."

"Nonsense," said Mark. "Women improve with age."

"You can't be trusted," Liz said. "You teach history. People who study the past think time passing is a good thing."

"Okay, okay, you guys." Robin waved her hands. "Gather around. Ivy, you've been such a great friend to me." She began to cry. "Sorry, sorry, everyone, it's the pregnancy."

"Happens a lot," said Phil.

"Now close your eyes, Ivy." Robin ducked into the kitchen.

With one hand covering my eyes, Mark led me to the couch and made me sit down. He smelled of freshly cut rose stems. "Ready?" he asked.

Before I had a chance to answer, Robin shoved a black kitten into my lap. He squirmed, and I lifted him with both hands. I held him out in front of me like a dirty diaper.

"Nice maternal instinct," Liz said, butting out her cigarette in the bottom of a mug.

"Are you allergic to cats?" Robin looked hurt. "He won't give you a rash or make you sneeze, will he? Don't worry about training him to use the litter box. Cats learn fast."

"No. I'm just in shock. Really. He's very cute. Thank you all so much." I passed the kitten to Mark. "Want to hold him?"

Mark pulled the furry little creature close to his neck. The kitten settled there, purring. He placed his two front paws over Mark's strong shoulder. Kept his back to me.

Good, I thought. *Just so we understand one another.*

I'd had pets before. I'd had fish and a hamster the first year that Cara lived with us. The hamster's coat was brown and white. His little wet nose was always twitching. His cage stood beside our beds. It smelled terrible: wood chips wet with hamster pee. My parents had given him to us both, but I thought of him as mine.

When Cara wasn't home, I would take him out of the cage. I'd sit him beside me on the bottom bunk and play with him. One day, when I reached inside the cage, he backed away. The next time I tried, he did the same thing. When I told Cara, she said, "He's just a stupid animal. His brain's no bigger than a grain of sand."

Then one day I saw Cara sitting on the bed with him, but she didn't see me. At first, she'd looked loving, soft. I imagined she'd looked that way with her dying mother's head in her lap. Then I saw she was holding the hamster too tightly, squeezing. His little beady eyes were almost popping out of his head. "I love you," she said while she squeezed him. "I love you to death."

I burst through the doorway. Cara just laughed that merry-go-round laugh of hers. Soon after, I found the animal dead in his cage. Mum said that's what happens to hamsters. They don't live very long. Their hearts just give out.

That memory flashed through my mind as I watched Mark pat the kitten's fur. "We talked of getting you a dog instead," said Robin. "But you have to walk dogs. They can't be left alone for long. A cat will be good company with less fuss."

I reached over to Mark's shoulder, where the kitten was half asleep. I scratched my new pet under his chin. "What shall I name you?" I said.

"The girl at the Humane Society said he was the smallest of the litter," said Phil. "Call him Runt."

"God, no!" Liz said. "He's black. Something about luck."

"I know, I'll call him Pluto," I said. "Pluto, like the cat in that creepy story by Edgar Allan Poe." I tried to lift the kitten away from Mark. Pluto opened his eyes and dug into Mark's shirt with his sharp claws.

"He's got a good grip for a little guy," Mark said. He pulled the kitten off and passed him to me.

"Get him de-clawed," said Liz with a tone of disgust. "He'll wreck your furniture."

I stroked Pluto all the way from his small head to his skinny tail. Felt how fragile his tiny neck was. He just stared me in the eyes, unsure about me. His tail was like a question mark.

✱

Not long after my party, Phil called to say that Robin had gone into early labour. The baby was coming weeks ahead of the due date. Mark and I jumped in a cab. We found Phil in a plastic seat in the hospital waiting room. He looked pale and shaken. "It'll be okay, man," Mark said, putting his arm around Phil.

As a doctor helping women to get pregnant, Phil was used to having power, playing with life. Now, I could see, he was scared. For the first time since we'd met, I felt close to him. I wished I'd let him take me out on a date after the taxi ride. I should have let him have his way with me. Maybe he wouldn't be with Robin now, and I would be getting all the attention.

Robin's doctor appeared, wearing his green scrubs. "The baby is fine," he told Phil. "Congratulations! You have a son. Five pounds, one ounce."

My heart squeezed. A headache started up. Phil and Robin had gone from being two people to being more than that. I was still only me. "I'll call Liz," I said. "She'll want to know."

Chapter Eight

I finally met little Jeremy a few days after he was born. His skin was pink and rubbery. He had pimples and thin fingernails. I could see veins through the skin on the top of his head. He seemed wide awake.

Sitting up in her hospital bed, Robin was trying to master the art of breast-feeding. "No one tells you it hurts!" she said.

Robin pointed to one corner of the room, by the window. "Did you see what Liz brought me this morning? She marched in and set it down on my head." Robin laughed. "Pass it to me, will you? There ... I'm sure I'm quite the sight in a pink plastic crown."

"I wish I had a camera," I said. "Mark would get a kick out of this."

"Mark, huh?" Robin winked. "I've been hearing rumours, Ivy."

"What do you mean?"

"He likes you, Phil said. I knew you'd be a good match."

"Did Mark say that?"

"Have you slept with him?" Robin asked. "Come on, Ivy. I want *every* detail. I'm an old married mother now."

"He's very nice."

"*Nice?* That's it?"

"Okay, sweet," I lied. "Gentle."

"Are you in love?"

"I don't know. How do you know?"

"Oh, you know."

✱

Before bed that evening, I brushed my teeth in front of the small bathroom mirror. My hair was rolled up on top of my head in a yellow towel. I was covered to the neck by the high collar of my robe. I stared at my small nose, my high cheekbones. My chin, as round as a heel. We'd never worn the same clothes, Cara and I. We didn't look alike. But

I could imagine that the towel draped around my head looked like long blonde hair. Like hers. Our eyes weren't that different. *We share a parent*, I told myself. If there was some of me in Cara, there was some of Cara in me. The fact sank in for the very first time, and I shivered.

In the middle of the night, I woke up curled into a tight ball under my covers. I felt like prey. I lay still, listening to Mark in the kitchen. He opened and closed the fridge. Ran some water, flipped the switch on the coffee maker.

"I've been working on what to tell my students," he said when I joined him. "Sorry if I woke you." He was leaning back against the counter, shirtless. His track pants hung from his narrow hips. His hair was messy. I wanted to reach out and run my fingers through those dark waves. I wanted to follow the black line of hair down his belly.

"Coffee?" he asked.

"Sure." I hadn't tied my robe properly, and the terry cloth hung open at the front. One of my breasts was exposed at the top. I moved to cover myself and tighten my belt.

"You're very beautiful when you're relaxed," Mark said. He reached out and stopped me from covering up. Then there was an emptiness about the air. A weightless, breath-taking quality to the space around us. It seemed to shrink, bringing us closer together. "Ivy, there's something I've wanted to do since we met." Mark leaned over, held my face in his hands and pulled it close. He kissed me hard on the lips. My lips, cheeks, all the way down my spine tingled. When you've waited too long, longer than normal, that's the way things are. Mark pulled me to him, lifted me in his arms. A moment later, Mark took my hand and led me into the bedroom.

In bed, I pretended I was an editor. I moved when Mark moved his body, and I did what he did, only more. I showed control. Then I let loose. Filled in the blanks. When Mark reached between my legs, I spread them. He pressed the palm of his hand into the small of my back, and I arched it. Mark tried to speak just before he came, but I caught his words on my tongue and kissed them away. *Everything has a natural story line, even sex*, I thought. *Sex is a fiction, too.*

Pluto sat on my dresser, a good distance away from the bed. He looked on, detached, the same way Dr. Stamp does in therapy. I had tried locking him out of the room (Pluto, not my shrink), but he just cried at the door. Mark said the kitten had bonded to me. Pluto thought I was his mother.

Twenty minutes later, we lay with Pluto purring between us.

"Why did you kiss me?" I asked.

Mark rolled towards me and began petting Pluto.

"Why wouldn't I? You're a mystery, and that's sexy." He leaned in and nibbled my bare shoulder. "Mmm, I love your smell."

"Really? I have a smell?"

I'm an average woman, with droopy breasts and thin, straight hair. My posture is poor. I have trouble keeping eye contact with others. What's attractive about that? Then I remembered something Liz once told me. "I guess I do have a nice rear end."

Mark laughed and grabbed me there.

After, we fell asleep together, naked. I dreamed of a flag flapping in the breeze. Fire eating its way up the pole.

When I woke hours later, I wanted to dance around the apartment. To shout out loud: I'm not a virgin anymore! I'd been released, stained, finally *marked.* Then a sense of horror came over me. *If I wasn't that girl with something to lose, who was I?*

Next thing I knew, my mind had floated away. I was lying in my sleeping bag beside Cara in a tent on the shore of Looking Glass Lake. Suddenly, she rolled right on top of me. She pinned me to the hard ground.

"Ivy," she'd said, "be dead for me."

"What?" I tried to push her away. "Get off!"

She made herself as heavy as possible. She held my arms at my sides with her hands. I was trapped. My head was free but the rest of me was stuck in the sleeping bag. "Come on, be dead for a minute," she said. There was a far-away look in her eye.

"No! Get off!"

Cara laughed and kissed me anyway. We hit our teeth together. I scrambled to move and shook my head.

"You'll like it. Hold still!"

The more I fought, the more she took charge. Her hands were inside my sleeping bag, under my pajamas, on my skin. Finally, I bit her lip as hard as I could. She screamed and rolled away. I felt a small piece of flesh in my mouth. I tasted blood on my tongue. She grabbed at her mouth and slapped me hard across the face. I struggled out of my sleeping bag and out of the tent. She chased me. The side of my head was pounding. I ran for my parents, but their canoe was gone, they were off somewhere. Cara laughed, a mean, scary laugh. I felt like dirt, and I wished she'd never been born!

I ran up to the edge of the cliff, where we'd sat earlier with Dad. I wanted to be rid of her. I wanted to walk down to the water and wash in the lake.

After that, Cara was inside me, whether she was present or not. Her flesh, her blood was mixed with my own. I'd swallowed her down.

I didn't tell Mark he wasn't really my first. Family doesn't count.

Chapter Nine

When Mark stayed late at the university, I waited up for him. I put his books in alphabetical order. Then I put them back as he'd had them. There were new piles of papers in the living room every time I came home. I cleared off the kitchen table for him to use as a desk. I dreaded September, when he would leave me to move into his condo.

I bought myself a few cookbooks and began to try out recipes on Mark. I did his laundry once. He seemed embarrassed, though, and asked me not to do it again. Sometimes I used his toothbrush or tried on his clothes. But I was careful. What if he came home and found me on the pullout couch in his best suit? Pretending he was there? I placed everything back exactly as I found it. I didn't want to scare him.

We never had *the* discussion. The one Liz used to call "Those three little words that kill all the fun." I practised in front of the bathroom mirror. I said it in as many different ways as possible. I love you. *I* love *you*. I *love* you. I wanted to see what he'd see when my mouth curled on the "l." Or whether I could say it, even to myself, without turning red. My heart raced.

I slept even less than usual with him next to me, but I could rest. I breathed slowly and evenly, floating over sleep, almost there. He smelled different after dark. I didn't want to miss that new smell. Sometimes he mumbled. Once, he said a word that sounded like "Yvonne." Another woman's name! I was furious. I gripped the pillow under my head, clenched my jaw. The next thing I knew I was under the sheets, between Mark's legs.

I woke him up to thoughts of only me.

Only me.

✳

One Saturday in mid-August, Mark propped himself up beside me in bed. "Ivy, guess what?"

I rolled over, rubbed sleep from my eyes.

"You can be rid of me sooner than we thought," he said. "I checked with the painters today. They're ahead of schedule. My condo will be ready next week."

I sat up. "Oh."

Mark undid my pajama top. He kissed my bare shoulder. "This gives me a chance to settle in before the term gears up."

"You don't have to go," I said. "I mean, you can stay as long as you like."

Mark pulled back. We hadn't talked about him staying on. As far as he knew, our deal was for a month. My ears filled with the sound of thunder. I felt a pounding that spread across my forehead, down into my chest. Then my blood thumped in my stomach. *How could I get him to stay?*

"Of course you should move into your own place," I said. I brushed a strand of hair away from my eyes. "See how dangerous it is to wake me? Never know who you'll find."

Mark laughed and slipped his hand under my pajama top. He squeezed my breast. "Come see the condo with me tomorrow?"

"Sure," I said, grinding my teeth. "It'll be fun."

I came down with a cold that evening. It turned into a full-blown fever, runny nose, the whole bit. I coughed. When Mark left the room, I stuck the thermometer under a light bulb to make my fever seem even higher. I was happy to see Mark worried. Not all of us have bubbly personalities like Robin. Or sit-up-and-say-hello tits like Liz. Not all of us can capture a man's attention easily. No, we aren't all pretty little stories that you can't put down. Some of us need to throw in some drama.

Mark was so sweet to delay moving out until I was better. The next day he carried the TV from the living room into my bedroom. Using one of my new cookbooks, he made carrot soup, which he served on a tray, with crackers. We ate in bed and watched scary movies that he'd rented. I stayed awake for the first movie in the *Omen* series, fell half asleep for *Jagged Edge*. I was out cold for most of *Dead Ringers*. That was fine. I'd seen them all before.

Being with Mark was the real comfort. Feeling his arm around me. I relaxed more than I had in months.

Chapter Ten

A couple of weeks later, Robin called off our regular Wednesday night dinner. It was the day after Liz and Rafe came back from their vacation in the south of France. Robin said she was sorry. She still felt run-down. Also, she wasn't comfortable breast-feeding in front of strangers. Yada yada yada. So Liz and I agreed to go to her place instead. *That's okay*, I told myself. *Maybe I'll learn more about Mark from Phil.*

I knocked and pushed open the unlocked door. The living room carpet was covered in brightly coloured toy animals. I stepped on a rubber shape that squeaked. The smell of mother's milk hung in the air. Liz was already there, tanned and healthy looking, sitting on the couch. Robin and Phil were in Jeremy's room, changing his diaper.

"The kid wet himself," Liz said. "Avoid that chair." She pointed to the large one with the dark spot on it. Then she patted the couch. "Sit by me. It's safe over here."

"I don't have to ask if you had a good time," I said.

"It was amazing," said Liz. "But I'm gone for two weeks and my office falls apart. I signed up a really good-looking guy, though. Noticed him writing a story on the beach. 'My fees are high,' I told him. 'I'm good.' Everything he writes is set in far-away places. Cha-ching! Count the markets."

Sometimes Liz reminds me of L'Oreal hair dye commercials. "It costs more," the models say. "But I'm worth it!" That's Liz. Full of herself, and yet worth every penny. Last year she held three publishing companies hostage for a week. They had to compete against each other for a book by one of her clients. Finally, she got that author a deal in the high six figures. It was in all the papers. Editors and publishers might not like her, but they sure as hell respect her.

"Hey, Ivy." Phil came into the room and kissed me on the cheek.

"Shouldn't you be at work?" I said.

"Yeah," said Liz. "Don't you have someone else to knock up?"

"I saw two women this morning," said Phil. "Robin wasn't happy about me going to work so soon after Jeremy was born. So I've just cut down my hours."

Robin walked into the room with Jeremy in her arms. She looked tired. She'd put on thirty-five pounds during her pregnancy. She was still wearing maternity pants. Under one breast, a wet spot on her T-shirt showed she was leaking milk.

Liz noticed the spot, too, and pointed. "God, will you look at that."

"This is the least of it," Robin said. Her hair was longer than I'd seen it before. She was wearing a scarf to keep her bangs off her face. Her grey roots showed, too.

"Let me have him, honey," Phil said, reaching for Jeremy.

Phil walked Jeremy back and forth across the living room. Jeremy's body had filled out, and he looked almost human. His eyelids fluttered. *What does an infant dream?* I thought. I couldn't imagine ever being that trusting. Seeing the baby like that disturbed me.

"Hire someone," Liz said. "Get a housekeeper for a while. Or a nanny. Christ, you can't be stuck in here. It's not normal."

"I'm fine."

Phil passed Jeremy back to Robin. "Chinese food okay?" Without waiting for an answer, he grabbed his jacket from a hook on the wall near the door. He patted his pockets, to make sure he had his wallet, and left.

Robin burst into tears. "Oh, you guys. I'm glad you came. I couldn't have gone out."

"Don't worry about it," Liz said. "My sister-in-law felt like a cow for months after she had her baby. It passes."

"No, it's not that," said Robin. "It's Phil. I think he's..." She bit her lip.

"Oh. My. God," said Liz.

Robin nodded. "I just know it."

"Know what?" I asked. "What are you two talking about?"

Liz rolled her eyes. "An affair, Ivy. She thinks Phil's having an affair."

"No way," I said. "You're just emotional these days."

Liz patted her breast pocket, looking for a package of cigarettes. "I can't believe I'm going to say this, but Ivy's right. Phil wouldn't. He's too…I don't know, under your thumb."

"Gee, thanks for your support, Liz," said Robin, sniffling. "You're the one person I thought I could count on to believe the worst." She looked at me. "At work, he has his face between women's legs all day long. What do I expect?"

"That's not fair," I said. "Phil's a doctor. He loves you."

Robin squeezed between Liz and me on the couch, holding Jeremy. "I smell perfume on his clothes when he comes home."

"Maybe there's a new nurse at his office," I said.

"He won't touch me, Ivy." Round, clear tears fell onto Jeremy's head. "He used to be all over me, and now, nothing. I'm lucky to get a peck on the cheek. We haven't slept together since…since…oh, I don't know." Robin cried harder. "Maybe since I was three months along. Look at me. I'm fat and ugly. This is supposed to be the best time of my life. I can't compete with some slut in size two outfits. Christ!" Robin wiped her nose on the back of her hand. "I'm going to ask him."

"I wouldn't do that," said Liz. "If it's true, it's just a phase. Whoever she is, she'll pass."

My jaw tightened and the muscles in my neck began to ache. "It's not true," I said. "Phil's different." I lifted Liz's brandy glass to my lips. I drank the golden liquid down in two gulps. It burned.

Robin cleared her throat. "I shouldn't have told you," she said. "I'm sorry. I can see I've made you uncomfortable."

"No, of course you haven't," I lied. "I just can't believe it, that's all. I don't want to believe it."

"Collect evidence," said Liz. "There are bound to be clues."

"I'm not getting a divorce, Liz!"

"Just in case."

What if Phil is cheating? I thought. What else could Robin do except ask him? Was she to wait silently until he came to his senses? Choke him? Stab him? Poison him to death?

Chapter Eleven

Mark came back to my apartment the next evening to get the last of his things. I was in the kitchen, digging in the cupboards. He shook the extra set of keys I'd given him in front of my nose. I ignored him.

"Robin's a mess," I said, ripping into a package of Japanese noodles. I began chopping green onion. "She thinks Phil's got another woman."

Mark pulled out a chair at the table and sat down. "He does."

I stopped chopping. "You knew and didn't say anything?"

"Look, Robin's your best friend. I didn't want to be in the middle."

"He's married, for Christ sake! They just had a kid."

"Whoa, why are you taking *my* head off?"

In his eyes, I saw anger and envy. I knew that look. It belonged to me.

"Oh, wow, you're jealous," I said. "I hear it in your voice. It's all over your face. You wish you were Phil, instead of being stuck here with me."

"What? That's crazy, Ivy. We're not even together." Mark walked out of the kitchen and into the living room. He tossed a few of his books into his bag.

I followed him. "We're good together," I tried more gently. "We belong together." I reached out to stroke his chest. "You feel it, too."

Mark jerked away from me. "I don't know what you think we've been doing, but it's over. You knew when we met that I'd only been single for a year. I don't want anything serious."

For a moment I almost felt sorry for Mark. His wife had left him. He'd been let go from his job. He knew how it felt to be second best, the last one picked. I nodded. "I know. You're right."

"Good." Mark zipped up his bag and headed for the door. "I'm glad you understand."

I went cold, as if Cara had stepped inside me from the beyond. *Yes, I understand,* I thought. It wasn't Cara I should have hated most all those years ago, it was our father. He was the one who'd turned his back on me and Mom. He was the one who'd said he loved us and lied. I looked at Mark and felt that old rage rising inside me again. He'd lied too, sort of. He'd let me think we were a real couple when we weren't.

I would talk to Dr. Stamp about my feelings next session. In the meantime, I knew what to do.

Cara had been careless. She always took chances. So, when I pushed her off the cliff, no one guessed the truth. Why should Mark's death make anyone suspect foul play? After all, Mark's peanut allergy was an accident waiting to happen.

"Wait," I said, in a soft voice. "This is all wrong. You can't leave on bad terms. We've had a good time together until now. I'm just shocked by Phil's affair. You're right, though. It's Phil I'm mad at, not you." I put my hand on Mark's arm. "Stay for dinner at least?" I forced a smile so rigid that I almost had to laugh.

In the living room, I poured red wine. We nibbled on cheese and crackers as we drank. Mark lit a joint, and I tried it. Soon the mood was relaxed and easy again. We cuddled on the couch with Pluto sitting across our laps. We listened to Leonard Cohen singing "First We Take Manhattan."

"Let me check on dinner," I said, breaking away. I returned with the half-empty wine bottle and topped up Mark's glass. I lit a candle and served supper on the coffee table. Then I watched the end of Mark's fork carry my noodle casserole to his tongue. I sat back in my chair and ate, smiling.

After about five minutes, Mark's face turned red. "Mind if I open a window?" he asked.

"Go ahead," I said with a nod. Maybe the problem is the pot we smoked."

He coughed. "No," he said, and reached for his throat. "Something's wrong. I can't breathe."

"I'll get you some water." I moved into the kitchen, ran the tap and returned with a glass. "Here." I held it out to him. Mark took a drink. Still gasping, he began to panic.

"Ivy. Really. I can't breathe. My throat." He pulled the collar of his shirt away from his neck. "Call 911." He staggered around. "Ivy, call an ambulance!" His face was turning purple.

"It's just a few peanuts," I said.

Mark looked at me, knowing. He tried to reach for the phone and fell to his knees.

I stood with my hands over my ears as he fell at the foot of my couch. He rolled about on the green shag rug, trying to breathe. He tried to plead with me but could only squeak out childish sounds. He lay there with his throat squeezing shut and couldn't shape words.

All at once, I felt a motherly urge to comfort him. I took my new nursing bra from the closet. As I undressed, I stood over Mark. He clawed at his neck. His eyes begged for help.

I slipped into the new bra and felt powerful. Like a woman. I knelt and lifted his head into my lap. Mark tried to fight back, but he was too weak.

"Why did you have to be like the others?" I said, rocking him. "All I wanted was to be yours. Your one and only."

I looked down at him in my arms. His eyes were wild and desperate. Sweat covered his face. His lungs could hardly work. I pressed his face into my breasts. Finally, he went limp.

I shuddered with desire. "I love you," I said, as he took his last breath.